Level 2

THE NATURE KIDS GUIDE TO SANDHILL CRANES

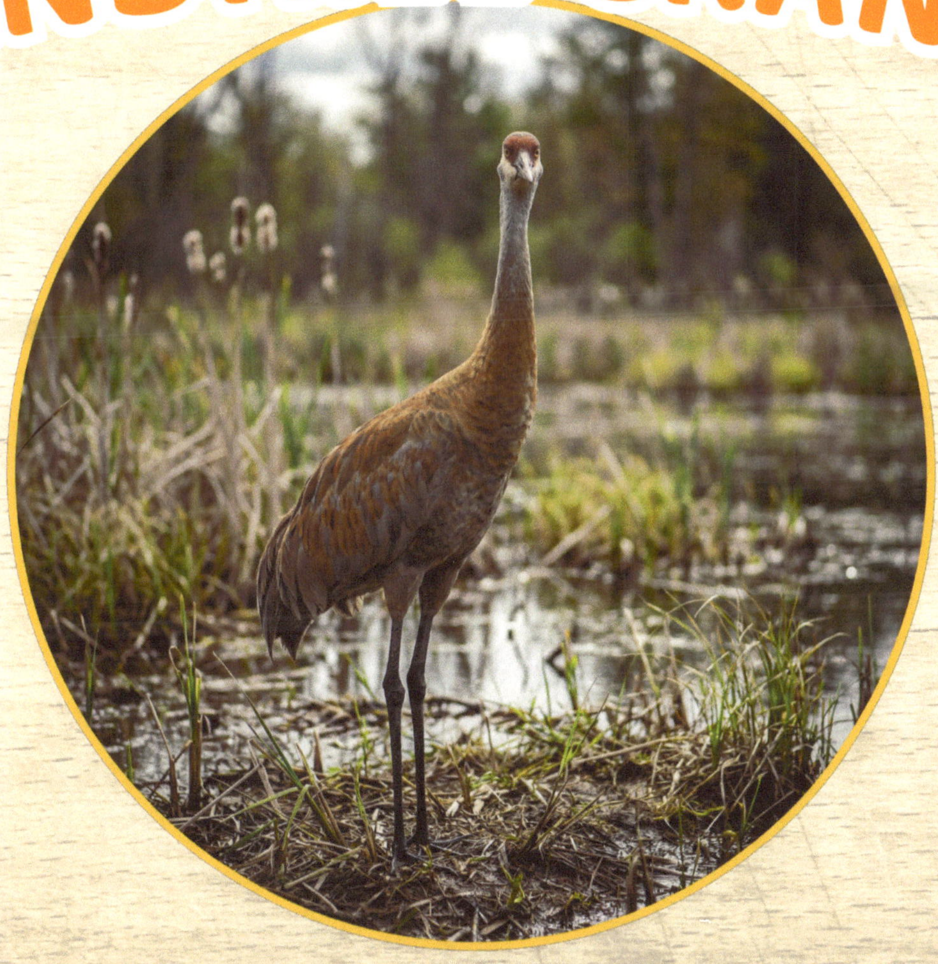

DAVID ANDERSON

LP Media Inc. Publishing
Text copyright © 2026 by LP Media Inc.
All rights reserved.

For information address LP Media Inc. Publishing,
30012 Variolite St NW, Princeton MN 55371
www.lpmedia.org

Publication Data

Sandhill Cranes
The Nature Kid's Guide to Sandhill Cranes — First edition.

Summary: "Learn all about Sandhill Cranes, the Nature Kid Way"
— Provided by publisher.

ISBN: 979-8-89818-150-5

[1. Sandhill Cranes – Non-Fiction] I. Title.

Title: The Nature Kid's Guide to Sandhill Cranes

CONTENTS

WETLAND WONDERS

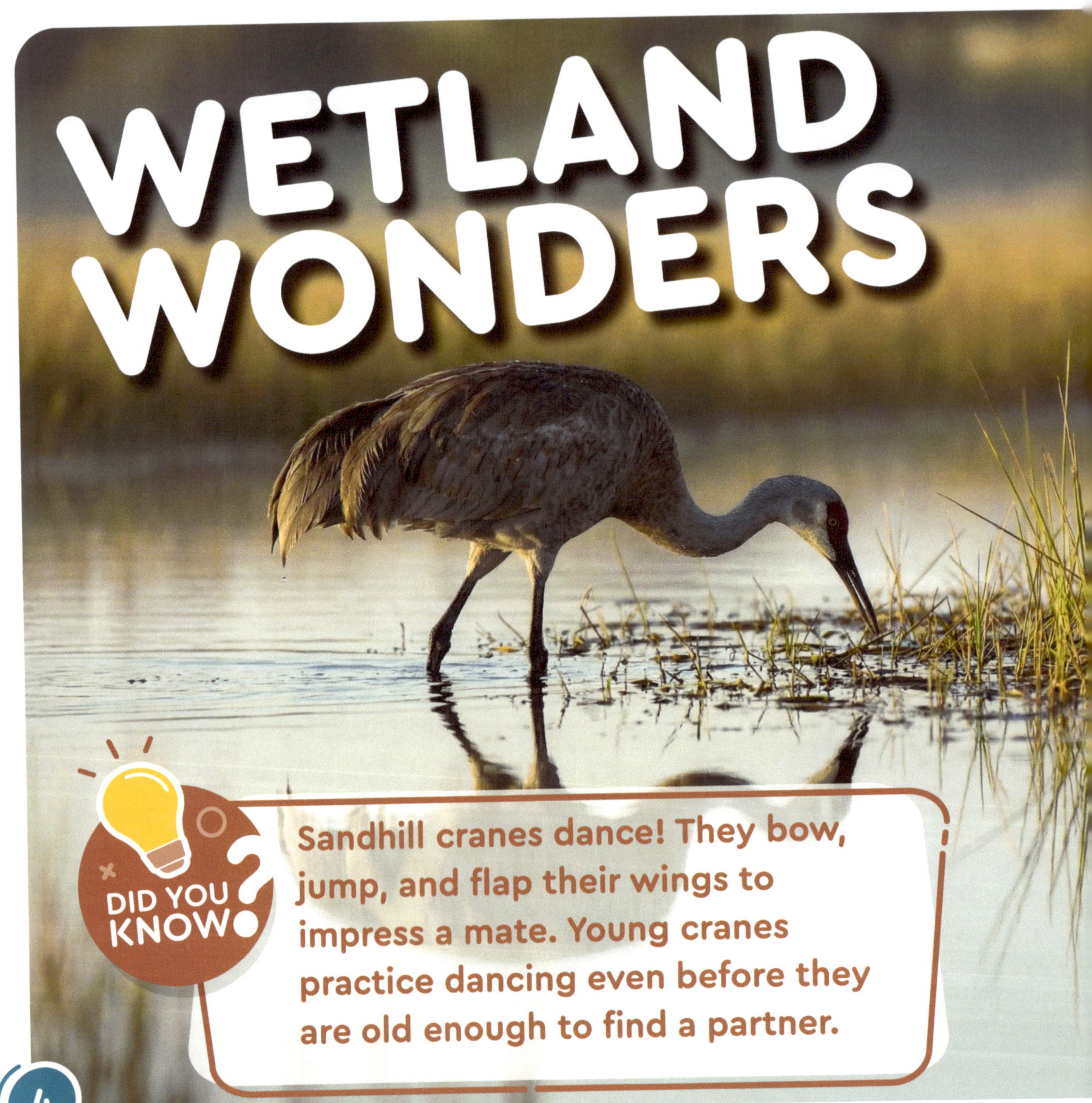

Sandhill cranes dance! They bow, jump, and flap their wings to impress a mate. Young cranes practice dancing even before they are old enough to find a partner.

Squawk! A tall gray bird wades through a marsh, searching for food.

Sandhill cranes live in **wetlands** like marshes, bogs, and meadows. These wet areas have the shallow water and soft ground that cranes need.

Wetlands give cranes everything they need. The water has food like snails and frogs. Tall grasses hide nests from danger. Their long legs help them walk through mud and water.

Sandhill cranes return to the same wetlands each year. Some wetlands freeze in winter, so the cranes fly south. This is called migrating.

COAST TO COAST

Whoosh! A crane flies over a golden prairie. Its wings stretch wide.

Sandhill cranes live across North America. They nest in Alaska, Canada, and many U.S. states. Some live as far south as Florida and Cuba.

In fall, most cranes **migrate** south. They fly to Texas, Mexico, and even further south. Some travel over 5,000 miles each year!

Each spring, over 500,000 cranes gather along Nebraska's Platte River. They stop there to rest on their long journey.

Florida sandhill cranes stay in Florida all year. They do not migrate like other cranes.

TALL BIRDS

Thump! A crane steps through tall grass. Its red crown bobs high.

Sandhill cranes are tall birds. They stand about 4–5 feet tall. That is around your height! Their long necks make them look even taller.

These large birds weigh between 6 and 14 pounds. Males are usually bigger than females.

Long legs help cranes stand above the tall grass. This makes it easy to spot danger coming.

Many of a sandhill crane's bones are hollow inside. This helps keep the bird light!

COOL CROWNS

Bow! A crane tilts its bright red head.

Sandhill cranes have a special patch on top of their heads. This patch is bare skin, not feathers, and it is bright red!

The red crown shows how a crane feels. When a crane gets excited, more blood flows to the patch. This makes the red color even brighter.

Young cranes do not have red crowns yet. Their heads are covered with rusty brown feathers. The red patch appears as they grow up.

A crane's red crown has tiny bumps called papillae. They make the color bright.

SHARP SENSES

Screech! A crane turns its head. Its keen eyes scan the marsh.

Sandhill cranes have excellent eyesight. They can spot a predator from far away.

Their eyes sit on the sides of their heads. This helps them see about 280 degrees around them, and watch for danger without turning.

Cranes also have good hearing. At night, they listen for predators sneaking through the marsh. Even the smallest splash in the water can wake a sleeping crane.

Cranes see more colors than humans can! They even see ultraviolet light.

BLENDING IN

Rustle! A gray crane stands still in dry grass. It almost disappears!

Sandhill cranes have gray feathers. This gray color can stand out in brown marshes. But these birds have a clever trick!

They rub mud on their feathers. The mud makes their gray feathers look brown. This helps them blend in with their surroundings.

Young cranes are different. They have rusty brown feathers. This color matches the grasses where they hide.

MUNCHING MEALS

Crunch! A crane snaps up a grasshopper with its long bill.

Sandhill cranes eat many different foods. They munch on plants, seeds, and grains. They also eat insects, snails, and small animals.

These birds change their diet with the seasons. In summer, they eat more protein like bugs and frogs to stay strong.

In fall and winter, cranes eat more grains. They visit farm fields to find corn and wheat. One crane can eat over a pound of food each day!

Cranes swallow small rocks to help grind the food inside their stomachs.

PROBE AND PECK

Cranes stomp their feet to scare bugs and worms into moving. Easy catch!

Snap! A crane jabs its beak into soft mud. It pulls out a snack!

Sandhill cranes use two main ways to find food. They probe and they peck. Each method helps them catch different meals.

To probe, a crane pushes its long bill into soft ground. It feels around for worms, roots, and tubers hiding below. The bill can reach about 4 inches deep.

To peck, a crane taps at food on the surface. It quickly grabs seeds, berries, and bugs this way. As cranes hunt, they walk slowly through fields. They watch the ground carefully for their next meal.

WATCH OUT
DID YOU KNOW?
Great horned owls can catch cranes at night while they sleep on the ground.

Swoosh! A coyote sneaks through the marsh. The cranes hear it just in time and fly away!

Sandhill cranes face danger from predators. Golden eagles hunt them from above. These fast, strong birds can dive down quickly.

Coyotes and foxes hunt cranes too. They sneak through tall grass to get close. Wolves may also attack cranes this way.

Bobcats are sneaky hunters too. They hide and wait for cranes to walk by. Young cranes and eggs are in the most danger. Raccoons will raid crane nests when the parents aren't around.

FIGHT BACK

Hiss! A crane spreads its wings wide. It faces a hungry fox.

Sandhill cranes can fight back when in danger. They spread their huge wings to look bigger. This can scare off predators.

Cranes kick with their strong legs. Their feet have sharp claws that make each kick hurt.

Cranes also jab with their pointed bills. They aim for eyes and faces. Adults fight hard to protect their chicks.

Sandhill cranes sometimes team up to mob predators, attacking from all sides at once.

SKY SAILORS

Wow! A sandhill crane soars high above the clouds.

Sandhill cranes are strong fliers. They travel long distances each year. Some fly over 5,000 miles!

Cranes use rising warm air called **thermals**. They circle up high on these air currents. This helps them save energy.

Sandhill cranes fly in large flocks. They form V shapes or long lines. They reach 35 miles per hour while flying.

Sandhill cranes can fly as high as 12,000 feet. That is more than two miles up in the sky!

DAYTIME DOINGS

Splash! A crane dips its bill in the water. The sun warms its gray feathers.

Sandhill cranes stay busy during the day. They spend many hours looking for food. Mornings are often the busiest time.

Cranes walk slowly through wetlands. They stop often to look and listen for danger.

In the afternoon, cranes may rest. They stand on one leg to save energy. They also preen their feathers to keep them clean.

Sandhill cranes may walk several miles in one day looking for food. They can cover two miles every hour!

FLOCK TOGETHER

Chirp! Hundreds of cranes gather in a field. Their calls fill the air.

Sandhill cranes are social birds. They like to be around other cranes, so they form large groups called flocks.

Flocks can be huge! Some have over 10,000 cranes. These big groups gather in safe places to sleep at night.

Cranes call to each other often. Their loud voices help the flock stay together and spot danger quickly.

Crane calls can be heard from two miles away! Their extra-long **windpipes** make their calls loud.

DANCING DUETS

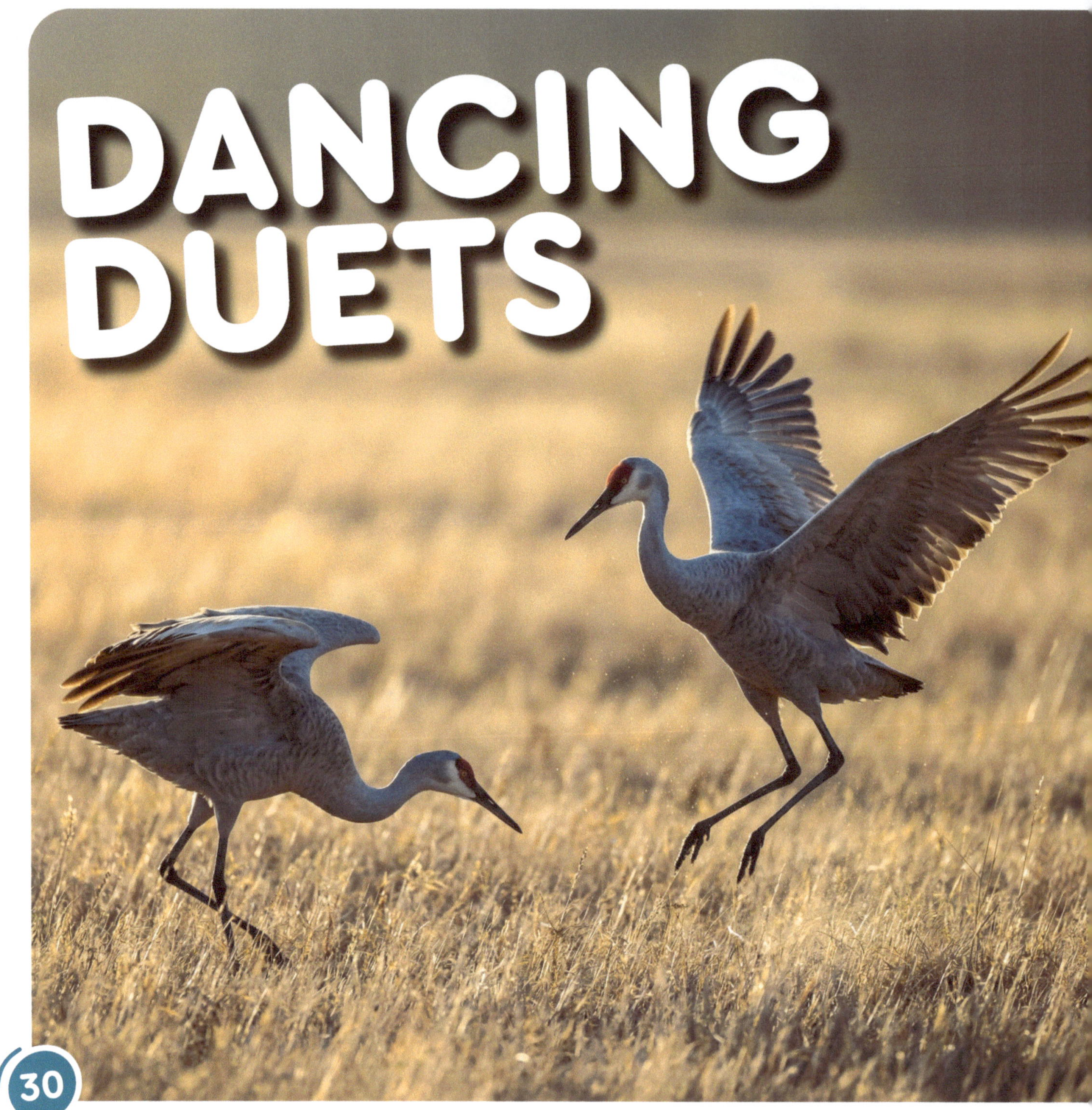

Flap! Two cranes leap and bow. Their dance begins.

Sandhill cranes are famous dancers. They jump, bow, and flap their wings. Both males and females dance together.

Dancing helps cranes form pairs. A pair may stay together for many years. They dance to strengthen their bond.

Cranes also toss sticks and grass into the air. Young cranes watch and practice too. They copy the moves of adult birds.

Crane pairs often return to the same dancing spot year after year for over a decade.

CUTE COLTS

Sandhill crane parents usually raise one or two colts each year. The chicks eat bugs and seeds.

Peep! A fuzzy chick waddles behind its parents. It stays close by and follows them everywhere.

Baby sandhill cranes are called colts. They hatch covered in soft brown fuzz. This color helps them hide in tall marsh grasses.

Colts can walk and swim within hours of hatching. They follow their parents wherever they go, and both parents help care for them.

Colts grow fast! They can fly when they are about 70 days old.

Young cranes then stay with their family for almost a year. This helps them learn important skills before living on their own.

FAMILY FIRST

Crane families can travel up to 500 miles in a single day!

Grunt! Two adult cranes walk side by side. A young colt follows close behind

Sandhill crane families are very close. It takes about a year for a colt to grow enough to be on it's own.

During this time, both parents protect their young. They watch for danger and chase away predators. The family eats and travels together.

Young cranes learn by watching their parents. They learn where to find food, the best places to rest, and the route for migration.

When fall comes, families migrate together. The young crane follows its parents south. This first trip teaches it the way.

COMEBACK CRANES

A crane lifts its head from the marsh. More cranes are nearby.

Long ago, sandhill cranes almost disappeared. Hunters killed many of them. Wetlands were drained for farms, leaving cranes with no home.

People worked hard to save them. Laws stopped the hunting. Wetlands were protected too.

Today, there are over 1 million sandhill cranes! Talk about a comeback!

Sandhill cranes are one of the oldest birds on Earth. Fossils show they lived over 2 million years ago!

SPOT A
CRANE

Buzz! A birdwatcher lifts binoculars. He spots a crane!

Sandhill cranes are easy to spot if you know when and where to look. They gather in huge groups during migration.

The best time to see them is spring or fall. Look near rivers, marshes, and farm fields. You can often see them driving by corn fields after harvest.

Listen for their loud calls. You can hear them from over 2 miles away!

FUN FACT!

Nebraska's Platte River hosts over 600,000 sandhill cranes each spring during migration!

GLOSSARY

wetlands
Wet, soggy places like marshes and bogs where water covers the ground.

migrate
To travel a long way from one home to another when seasons change.

windpipes
The tube inside the throat that carries air to and from the lungs..

thermals
Bubbles of warm air that rise up into the sky.

papillae
Tiny bumps on skin that can make colors look bright.